Scratch's **BAD** Reputations

T0362637

assisted by
Ali Sparkes

Hi, I'm
Scratch!

Give them a chance!

"It takes all sorts of animals to make the wild world work and every creature in this book has a very important job to do.

I hope that by learning a bit more about them, you'll learn to love them, too. An animal doesn't have to be cute and cuddly to matter – so join Scratch and champion these important underdogs!"

– Chris Packham, nature expert

OXFORD
UNIVERSITY PRESS
AUSTRALIA & NEW ZEALAND

Oxford University Press is a department of the University of Oxford.

It furthers the University's objective of excellence in research, scholarship, and education by publishing worldwide. Oxford is a registered trademark of Oxford University Press in the UK and in certain other countries.

Published in Australia by
Oxford University Press
Level 8, 737 Bourke Street, Docklands, Victoria 3008, Australia

First published 2014
This edition 2019
Reprinted 2020, 2021 (twice)

ISBN 9780190318291

Series Editor: Nikki Gamble
Illustrations by Ross Collins
Printed in China by Leo Paper Products Ltd

Links to third party websites are provided by Oxford in good faith and for information only. Oxford disclaims any responsibility for the materials contained in any third party website referenced in this work.

Acknowledgements

The publishers would like to thank the following for the permission to reproduce photographs:
Cover photos: Michael Patrick O'Neill/Alamy; pistolseven/Shutterstock; Super Prin/Shutterstock; natrot/Shutterstock
p4: Michael Patrick O'Neill/Alamy; **p6t**: D. Kucharski K. Kucharska/Shutterstock; **p6b**: Ivelin Radkov/Shutterstock; **p8t**: MaxyM/Shutterstock; **p8b**: Paul Fell/Shutterstock; **p9t**: Aso Fujita/Amana images Inc./Alamy; **p9b**: alle/Shutterstock; **p11**: Paul Souders/Corbis; **p12**: Rob Hainer/Shutterstock; **p13**: Claud Nuridsany & Marie Perennou/Science Photo Library; **p14-15**: Barry Mansell/Naturepl; **p16**: arka38 /Shutterstock; **p17**: Arnoud Quanjer/Shutterstock; **p18-19**: Flash-ka/Shutterstock; **p20**: Michiel de Wit/Shutterstock; **p21t**: Wichan Kongchan/Shutterstock; **p22b**: Galyna Andrushko/Shutterstock; **p22t**: Kuttelvaserova Stuchelova/Shutterstock; **p22b**: Simon Tilley; **p24**: Kuttelvaserova Stuchelova/Shutterstock.

Background images
Robert_s/Shutterstock; schankz/Shutterstock; Rich Carey/Shutterstock; AlinaMD/Shutterstock; Jovana Milanko/Shutterstock; Viachaslau Kraskouski/Shutterstock; Oliver Sved/Shutterstock.

We have made every effort to trace and contact all copyright holders before publication. If notified, the publisher will rectify any errors or omissions at the earliest opportunity.

Contents

It's not fair! And it's not just me. There are lots of animals making humans scream, but we just want to be loved!

So *try* not to panic, and read on. Could you stop screaming now?

Shark Shock

HORROR STORY: A great white shark glides through the shallow water. Someone goes swimming. A dark fin pokes up through the waves.

Then there's lots of kicking and screaming and ... well, I don't want to put you off your jam tart.

So – why stick up for sharks?

Well, they're not *that* bad. OK, they *do* kill about 15 people a year – but mostly by mistake. Divers and surfers look a bit like tasty seals. Sharks sometimes get confused and chew on them.

If someone walked by now, looking just like a bit of cake, *you* might bite *them* ...

So what's more dangerous than a shark?

Um ... stairs.

Yes, when it comes to stairs, you humans are hopeless. Hundreds of people are killed falling down stairs every year. You should grow a tail for balance, like me!

SCRATCH FACT

Some sharks can smell a single drop of blood in an area of water the size of a swimming pool.

SCRATCH TIP

Don't put a shark in your swimming pool.

Roaches Rock!

Nothing SCUTTLES like a cockroach ... into houses, into hotels ... making humans scream!

But why? Cockroaches don't bite. But they'll scoff anything. In fact, they're a *lot* like you. They *are!* Scientists say they love lollies so much, they dribble when they smell them.

(And now you're dribbling, too. Ugh. Please stop it.)

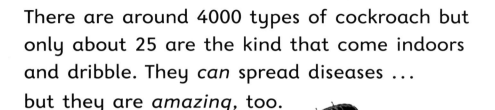

There are around 4000 types of cockroach but only about 25 are the kind that come indoors and dribble. They *can* spread diseases ... but they are *amazing*, too.

Don't believe me?
Check out these facts!

SCRATCH FACT

The Madagascan hissing cockroach is like a walking set of bagpipes. It has holes down its body and it squeezes air through them, making a hissing sound.

SCRATCH FACT

Some cockroaches can survive without food for six weeks or more. And scientists have shown that some cockroaches can live without their *heads* for two weeks.

SCRATCH TIP

Don't try to live without your head for two weeks. It doesn't work for humans.

7

Wonderful Wasps

"WONDERFUL wasps?! Are you completely, eyeball-poppingly BONKERS?!" you shout.

Calm down. And stop making that face!

Fair enough – wasps can:

- fly around your face
- angrily head-butt windows when trapped indoors
- bring their mates to your picnic without asking
- sting.

SCRATCH FACT

Nearly all wasps are female and they're the ones that sting.

Wasps are also the insect world's most talented **architects**. Here's what they can build with bits of wood that they've chewed up and spat out:

Here's a wasp house – beautiful, eh?

Wasps helpfully **pollinate** plants. Wasps are food for birds. And – when you look at them closely – wasps are quite good-looking.

SCRATCH TIP

Don't flap at a wasp today. Sing a song and back away.

Go on – admit it. I'm pretty.

9

Stupendous Stingrays

Do you like swimming? I do. Rats are awesome swimmers. Now meet an even *better* swimmer.

STINGRAYS! They hide in the sand on the seabed, then whoosh up and flap through the water like weird birds. Stingrays have a nasty sting on their tails.

SCRATCH FACT

Stingrays hunt by smell and feel. Their eyes are on top of their heads so they can detect predators above them.

Don't try this at home!

OK – they *have* killed people.

But nowhere near as many as sharks – and stairs. (*Remember those killer stairs?!*)

There are around 200 different types of stingray. They can be as small as a child's hand or bigger than an adult! Stingrays eat crabs and shellfish.
They are quite shy, although some stingrays will let divers hand-feed them. In aquariums, some stingrays even swim up to get their backs scratched!

SCRATCH TIP

Don't try to hide in sand on the seabed unless you're a stingray.

And if you *are* a stingray, *what* are you doing reading this book?! The pages will get soggy!

Webby Wonders

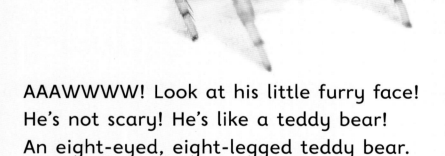

AAAWWWW! Look at his little furry face!
He's not scary! He's like a teddy bear!
An eight-eyed, eight-legged teddy bear.

But here in Australia, maybe you *should* be
scared of spiders.

Sydney funnel-web spiders have fangs that can
bite right through a toenail. They are one of
the world's deadliest spiders. There's **anti-venom**
for their bite, though, so most human victims survive.

Spiders don't *want* to bite you. They want to bite insects. Would *you* prefer to bite a doughnut ... or an elephant?

A doughnut, right! But you *might* bite an elephant if it stood on your head. See the spider's point now?

Many spiders eat flies. If they didn't, there would be swarms of flies everywhere. And spiders make *beautiful webs* –

look!

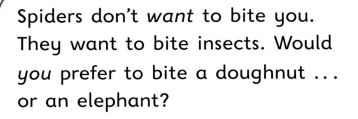

SCRATCH FACT

Some people in Cambodia eat fried tarantula spiders. Yum!

SCRATCH TIP

A bit of garlic makes fried tarantula extra tasty.

13

Fang Fear

VAMPIRE BATS!
Mwahahahaha!
(Do your best scary voice
for this bit):

By moonlight they swarm in
search of blooooooood! Swooping
down on your neck, getting out
their huge fangs and ...

OK! *Stop!*

That's not true. That's just in horror films.

In *real* life, vampire bats crawl about in
the grass and then fly up and land on
an animal's bottom, such as a cow, horse
or donkey. Next, with their teeny-weeny
fangs, they make a tiny cut. The animal
they bite doesn't usually notice.

SCRATCH TIP

Don't bite a
cow's bottom.
It *will* notice.

14

"Isn't the body *completely drained of blood?!*" I hear you scream.

Nope – vampire bats drink about a teaspoonful. Then they're full.

"But they carry diseases!" I hear you whimper.

Well, they *can*. But so can your dog or cat.

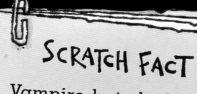

SCRATCH FACT

Vampire bats look after each other. If one is sick and hungry, another bat will pass along some blood. (*You don't want to know how ...)*

15

Sensational Scorpions

What ARE scorpions? Are they spiders? Mini lobsters? No. They are **arachnids**, like spiders, because they have eight legs. But *where* did they get those claws and stinging tails?!

OK. I admit it. I'm *rat*tled. (Hold my paw.) Scorpions *are* freaky. They live almost everywhere — from deserts to rainforests and even in some cities.

Out of almost 2000 different types, only 30 or 40 have stings that can kill you. These scorpions *do* kill thousands of people every year, when they're cornered or feel threatened.

SCRATCH FACT

Some scorpions can live on just one insect a year.

16

So why are scorpions sensational?

Some types of scorpion can survive being frozen solid! After the scorpion defrosts, it just walks away.

Noisy Devils

Life's tough when you look
and sound WEIRD.

And everyone calls you a *devil*.

And you smell of **decay**.

You're not going to get invited
to many parties.

Tasmanian devils are **carnivores**.
They're **marsupials** that live
in Tasmania. They make wild
shrieking noises that scare the
pants off people.

When a Tasmanian devil gets
upset, its ears go red. Then it
lets off a stink like rotting meat.

SCRATCH FACT

A Tasmanian devil
stores fat in its tail.
A skinny tail means
it's unwell.

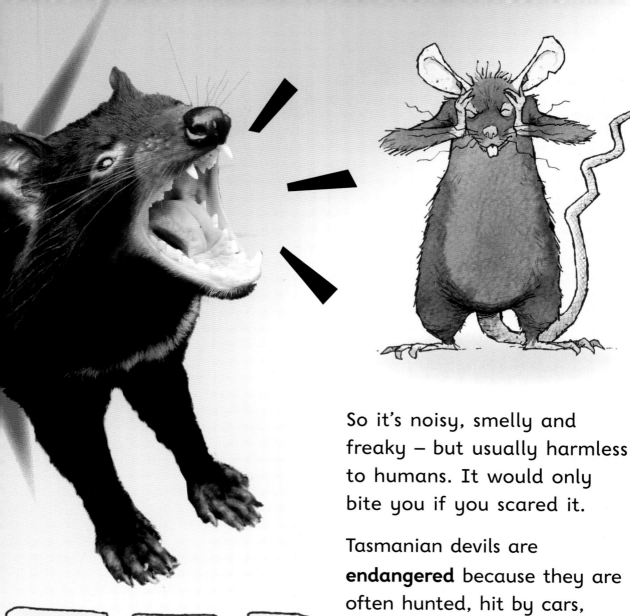

So it's noisy, smelly and freaky — but usually harmless to humans. It would only bite you if you scared it.

Tasmanian devils are **endangered** because they are often hunted, hit by cars, or they suffer from diseases. There are so few left now that they're protected by law.

Poor devils.

SCRATCH TIP

If you want to get asked to parties, try *not* to scream or make your ears go red.

Snake Shake

AAARRRRGH!

I admit it. I'm scared of snakes. But I'm a *rat!* A snake sees me and thinks, "Ooh – munchies!"

How scared should *you* be? If they bite, snakes can inject venom, which is painful and can sometimes be deadly.

So why am I sticking up for snakes? They'd eat me! Well ... snakes don't *mean* to be mean. They've got to eat *something*. And did you know that scientists think snake venom could be used to make *medicine?* Truly! One day you might get *cured* by a snake!

And look – some snakes are quite pretty.

But being this pretty can mean you end up as a shoe or a purse. Many thousands of snakes are killed every year just for their beautiful skin.

SCRATCH TIP

Never wake a snake.

SCRATCH FACT

Snakes don't have eyelids. (That made you blink, didn't it?)

Clap the Rat!

Aaawwwww, come on!
Give me some applause.

LOOK AT ME.

I'm cute.

Some people say rats are smelly and carry diseases. But I carry no more diseases than other wild animals. I'm clean, I am! Of course, some of my wild rat mates think *you're* smelly. They might bite – so don't mess with them.

But some of us live with humans. Ali Sparkes (*my assistant on this book*) has kept pet rats and says they're as clever and friendly as dogs.

See?

So – are you *still* going to do a flappy-shrieky dance whenever a wasp wafts by?

Will you go weak or freak and squeak, "Eeek!" when you see a spider?

Even after everything I've told you? *Or* will you say, "It's not *bad*. It's just got a bad *reputation*."

I hope you do.
Especially about rats.
You *do* think I'm cute really.
You do. You *doooooooooooo!*
Rub my ears. You know you want to ...

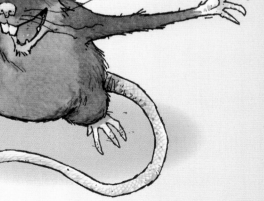

Glossary

anti-venom: a special medicine made to cure you if you're bitten by a snake, a spider or a scorpion

arachnids: animals with eight legs such as spiders and scorpions

architects: people who design buildings

carnivores: animals that eat meat

decay: rot or slowly break down

endangered: when all the animals of one kind are in danger of dying; this type of animal would not exist anymore

marsupials: animals that carry their babies around in a pouch (like kangaroos)

pollinate: to put pollen from one flower into another flower. This helps new flowers to grow.

reputation: what people think about a person or thing

ultraviolet: a kind of light that makes certain things glow in the dark

Index